of co-operation
is both valuable and
important to a child's later
development, and this is found,
for instance, in *Finger Rhymes*,
the first book of the eight book series.

This series provides an enjoyable intro-
duction to poetry, music and dance for
every young child. Most books of this
type have only a few rhymes for each
age group, whereas each book of this
series is intended for a particular age
group. There is a strong teaching sequence
in the selection of rhymes, from the
first simple ways of winning the child's
interest by toe tapping and palm
tickling jingles, through practice in
numbers, memory and pronunciation,
to combining sound, action and
words. For the first time young
children can learn rhymes
in a sequence that is
related to their age.

•❧O❧•

Contents

LEARNING WITH TRADITIONAL RHYMES

Dancing Rhymes

by DOROTHY TAYLOR

with illustrations by
MARTIN AITCHISON, FRANK HUMPHRIS
and BRIAN PRICE THOMAS
and photographs by JOHN MOYES

Ladybird Books Loughborough

Did you ever see a lassie

Did you ever see a lassie,
A lassie, a lassie,
Did you ever see a lassie
Go this way and that?

Go this way and that way,
And this way and that way.
Did you ever see a lassie
Go this way and that?

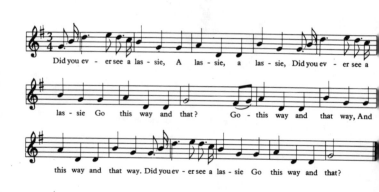

Did you ev - er see a las - sie, A las - sie, a las - sie, Did you ev - er see a las - sie Go this way and that? Go - this way and that way, And this way and that way. Did you ev - er see a las - sie Go this way and that?

Verse 1: One child performs an action in centre of ring whilst other children watch.

Verse 2: Everyone imitates her action.

(The word 'laddie' can be substituted for 'lassie' throughout this rhyme.)

Oh, the grand old Duke of York

Oh, the grand old Duke of York,
He had ten thousand men,
He marched them up to the top of the hill,
And he marched them down again.

And when they were up they were up,
And when they were down they were down,
And when they were only half-way up,
They were neither up nor down.

Oh, the grand old Duke of York, He had ten thou-sand men, He marched them up to the top of the hill, And he marched them down a - gain. And when they were up they were up, And when they were down they were down, And when they were on - ly half - way up, They were nei - ther up nor down.

Children stand in a line across the room.

Verse:
lines 1 and 2, march on the spot;
line 3, advance marching;
line 4, march backward.

Chorus:
line 1, march forward;
line 2, march backward;
lines 3 and 4, march forward with tiny steps.

Here we go Looby Loo

Here we go Looby Loo,
Here we go Looby Light,
Here we go Looby Loo,
All on a Saturday night.

You put your right arm in,
You put your right arm out,
You shake it a little, a little,
And turn yourself about.

Here we go Looby Loo, etc.

You put your *left arm* in, etc.
Here we go Looby Loo, etc.

You put your *right leg* in, etc.
Here we go Looby Loo, etc.

You put your *left leg* in, etc.
Here we go Looby Loo, etc.

You put your *whole self* in, etc.
Here we go Looby Loo, etc.

Here we go Loo - by Loo, Here we go Loo - by Light,

Here we go Loo - by Loo, All on a Sa-tur-day night. You

put your right arm in————, You put your right arm out etc.

During chorus, children skip round in a ring. They stand still whilst singing the verse and fitting the actions to the words, turning round rapidly whilst singing the last line.

On the bridge at Avignon

On the bridge at Avignon,
They are dancing, they are dancing,
On the bridge at Avignon,
They are dancing in a ring.

The gentlemen bow this way,
And then again bow this way.

On the bridge at Avignon, etc.

The ladies curtsey this way,
Again they curtsey this way.

On the bridge at Avignon, etc.

*All children skip round
in a ring during the chorus.
During the verse they
perform the appropriate
action.*

11

The farmer's dog's at my back door

The farmer's dog's at my back door,
His name is Bobby Bingo,
B I N G O, (*spell out*)
B I N G O,
B I N G O,
And Bingo is his name O.

Children join hands to form a ring. They dance round a child who stands in the middle. At the spelling out of BINGO, they all stand still and the child in the centre points to a child who should shout out 'B' and to another who shouts 'I', and so on. The child who shouts out 'O' is the next one into the centre.

The farm - er's dog's at my back door, His name is Bob - by Bin - go,

B. I. N. G. O., B. I. N. G. O.,

B. I. N. G. O., And Bin - go is his name O.

13

When I was a young girl, a young girl, a young girl

When I was a young girl,
    a young girl, a young girl,

When I was a young girl,
    how happy was I.

And this way and that way,
    and this way and that way,

And this way and that way,
    and this way went I.

Hold out dresses, step to left, step to right.

When I was a young girl, a young girl, a young girl, When I was a young girl, how hap-py was I. And this way and that way, and this way and that way, And this way and that way, and this way went I.

When I was a schoolgirl,
    a schoolgirl, a schoolgirl,

When I was a schoolgirl,
    how happy was I.

And this way and that way,
    and this way and that way,

And this way and that way,
    and this way went I.

Hands together to form book.

When I was a teacher,
    a teacher, a teacher, etc.

Pointing to blackboard.

When I had a sweetheart,
    a sweetheart, a sweetheart, etc.

Throwing a kiss.

When I had a husband,
    a husband, a husband, etc.

Arm in arm.

When I had a baby,
    a baby, a baby, etc.

Nurse in arms.

Children join hands to form a ring. They all dance round singing words of first two lines of each verse. Then they stand still, unclasp hands and continue singing whilst performing the action mentioned beneath each verse.

Here we go round the mulberry bush

Here we go round the mulberry bush,
The mulberry bush, the mulberry bush,
Here we go round the mulberry bush,
On a cold and frosty morning.

This is the way we wash our hands,
Wash our hands, wash our hands,
This is the way we wash our hands
On a cold and frosty morning.

Here we go round, etc.

This is the way we *wash our face* . . .

. . . *comb our hair*

. . . *tie our shoes*

. . . *go to school*

Chorus: All children skip round in a ring, holding hands.
Verse: They stand still and perform the action.

Here we go round the mul - berry bush, The mul - berry bush, the mul - berry bush,

Here we go round the mul - berry bush , on a cold and frost - y morn - ing .

19

The leaves are green

The leaves are green, the nuts are brown,
They hang so high they won't come down,
Leave them alone till frosty weather,
Then they will all come down together.

*The players dance in a circle clockwise, flopping down to
the ground on the last line. Sing again, dancing in an
anti-clockwise direction. Repeat at will.*

The leaves are green, the nuts are brown, They hang so high they won't come down,

Leave them a - lone till fros - ty wea-ther, Then they will all come

down to - geth - er.

21

Here comes a blue-bird through the window

Here comes a blue-bird through the window,
Here comes a blue-bird through the window,
Here comes a blue-bird through the window,
High diddle dum day.

Take a little dance and a hop in the corner,
Take a little dance and a hop in the corner,
Take a little dance and a hop in the corner,
High diddle dum day.

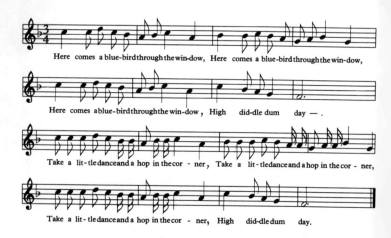

Here comes a blue-bird through the win-dow, Here comes a blue-bird through the win-dow,

Here comes a blue-bird through the win-dow, High did-dle dum day — .

Take a lit-tle dance and a hop in the cor - ner, Take a lit-tle dance and a hop in the cor - ner,

Take a lit-tle dance and a hop in the cor - ner, High did-dle dum day.

The children form a ring with clasped hands and raised arms. Girl enters ring and she is called 'blue-bird', 'yellow-bird', etc., according to the colour of her dress.

At end of verse 1 she chooses a partner and waltzes off with her, singing the words of verse 2. Then chosen partner starts game again.

You put your left arm out

You put your left arm out,
Your left arm in,
Left arm out and shake it all about,
You do the Cokey Cokey
      and turn around,
That's what it's all about.

Oh, do the Cokey Cokey,
Oh, do the Cokey Cokey,
Oh, do the Cokey Cokey,
Knees bend, arms stretch,
Ra Ra Ra.

You put your *right arm* out,
Your *right arm* in, etc.

Oh, do the Cokey Cokey, etc.

You put your *left leg* out, etc.

Oh, do the Cokey Cokey, etc.

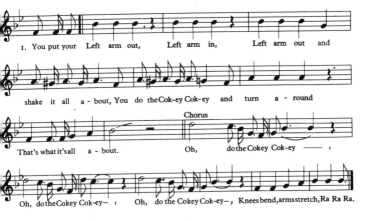

1. You put your Left arm out, Left arm in, Left arm out and shake it all a-bout, You do the Cok-ey Cok-ey and turn a-round That's what it's all a-bout.

Chorus

Oh, do the Cokey Cok-ey ——, Oh, do the Cokey Cok-ey ——, Oh, do the Cokey Cok-ey—, Knees bend, arms stretch, Ra Ra Ra.

Written by Jimmy Kennedy. Copyright by Kennedy Music Co. Ltd. London.
Reproduced by permission of Campbell Connelly & Co. Ltd., London.

You put your *right leg* out, etc.

Oh, do the Cokey Cokey, etc.

You put your *whole self* out, etc.

Oh, do the Cokey Cokey, etc.

Verse: *A circle is formed and children perform the actions of the verse. At line 4—do the Cokey Cokey—put fingertips to fingertips and rock arms from side to side, then turn around.*

Chorus: *Lines 1-3*
All join hands and advance to meet in the middle then retreat.

Line 4:   *Release hands, bend knees, stretch arms.*

Line 5:   *Stamp feet alternately.*

O, have you seen the muffin man

O, have you seen the muffin man,
The muffin man, the muffin man;
O, have you seen the muffin man
Who lives in Drury Lane O?

O yes, I've seen the muffin man,
The muffin man, the muffin man;
O yes, I've seen the muffin man
Who lives in Drury Lane O.

Players join hands to form a ring.
One child is blindfolded and stands
in the centre with a stick or rolled
newspaper in his hand.

Everyone sings the QUESTION verse.
At the end the blindfolded player touches
someone in the ring. This person sings
the RESPONSE verse at the end of which
the blindfolded child guesses who it can be.

If correct, the two children change places and
the game can begin again.

O, have you seen the muf-fin man, The muf-fin man, the muf-fin man; O,
have you seen the muf-fin man Who lives in Dru-ry Lane O?

A-hunting we will go

A-hunting we will go,
A-hunting we will go,
We'll catch a fox
And put him in a box,
And never let him go.

*Two lines of children face each other to form a wide lane.
At the top of the line, the two children facing each other join
hands and slip-step sideways down to the end of the lane and
back to the top whilst the rest of the children sing and clap
rhythmically.*

*The dancing couple loose hands and skip round the back
of their own lines, the rest of the children following behind.*

*At the bottom, the leaders join hands to form an arch whilst
the other children meet their partners, joining hands and
going under the arch to reform lines with a new top couple
ready to start again.*

The game goes on until all children have had a turn.

A —— hunt - ing we will go ——, A—hunt - ing we will

go,—— We'll catch a fox And put him in a box, And ne - ver let him go.

Skip, skip, skip to my Lou

Skip, skip, skip to my Lou,
Skip, skip, skip to my Lou,
Skip, skip, skip to my Lou,
Skip to my Lou, my darling.

Partner's gone, what will I do?
Partner's gone, what will I do?
Partner's gone, what will I do?
Skip to my Lou, my darling.

Skip, skip, skip to my Lou, etc.

Two circles are formed, one inside the other, boys on the inside, girls on the outside. Each faces his partner, holding hands.

Chorus: All skip round.

Verse 1: Girls stand still whilst boys skip round.

Chorus: Each boy takes a new partner and game continues as before.

Skip, skip, skip to my Lou, Skip, skip, skip to my Lou,

Skip, skip, skip to my Lou, Skip to my Lou, my dar - ling.

I had a little dog and his name was 'Buff'

I had a little dog and his name was 'Buff',
I sent him up the street for a pennyworth of snuff,
He broke my box and spilt my snuff
I think my story's long enough.

It isn't you, it isn't you, . . . but it's you!

I had a lit-tle dog and his name was 'Buff', I sent him up the street for a penny worth of snuff, He broke my box and spilt my snuff I think my sto-ry's long en-ough.

Children stand in a ring,
one skipping round the outside.
On the last 'you', the chosen one
touches another child on the shoulder
and they both race in opposite
directions to fill the gap.

(A variation of
'I Sent A Letter To My Love'.)

I sent a letter to my love

I sent a letter to my love
And on the way I dropped it;
One of you has picked it up
And put it in your pocket.

All children except one sit down in a ring.
The chosen one runs round the outside whilst
the song is sung and drops a handkerchief behind
one of the seated children on the word 'pocket',

I sent a let-ter to my love And on the way I dropped it; One of you has picked it up And put it in — your pock-et.

*whereupon both children race round
the outside of the circle in opposite directions
and try to get to the empty space first.
The loser becomes the new soloist.*

We'll hire a horse and steal a gig

We'll hire a horse and steal a gig,
And all the world shall have a jig,
And we'll do everything we can
To push the business on.

To push the business on
To push the business on
And we'll do everything we can,
To push the business on.

Verse: Dance round in a ring.
Chorus: Face a partner, clap own hands and then
partner's to end of chorus. Repeat at will.

We'll hire a horse and steal a gig, And all the world shall have a jig, And
we'll do ev'ry-thing we can to push the busi-ness on. To
push the busi-ness on — To push the busi-ness on — And
we'll do ev'ry-thing we can, To push the busi-ness on —

Sally go round the moon

Sally go round the moon,
Sally go round the stars,
Sally go round the chimney pots
    on a Sunday afternoon. Oop.

. . . on a *Monday* afternoon, etc.

*Children all join hands in a ring and dance round in a
clockwise direction. At 'Oop', the right leg is kicked up as
high as possible. For the next verse, kick left leg and dance
in the opposite direction.*